Title:

I0141794

Common Hoof Problems, how to treat and beat them: A guide for the horse owner.

Disclaimer:

As with all horse related activities, all techniques suggested in this guide are to be approached with caution since horses can be unpredictable and may have different reactions. It is always a good idea to consult a professional/ specialist if you are unsure about any of the aforementioned exercises. The author will not be responsible for, nor will accept any liability for any injury or loss incurred.

"*Farrier-Friendly*"™ publication

Published by:

FARRIER-FRIENDLY™ SERVICES

Athens, OH 45701

Website: www.farrierfriendly.com
Email: farrierfriendly@hotmail.com

Book cover design by Bryan Farcus

Table of Contents:

Preface :

For most horse owners, there is nothing more exasperating than a hoof problem. As the old saying goes, "if you've got no hoof, you have no horse". Fortunately, this doesn't apply to every hoof problem, as many are preventable, if addressed early enough.

As a practicing farrier, one of my most powerful tools to help horse owners overcome hoof problems is education. It is imperative that as farriers we allow enough time in our busy schedules to sit down and discuss any concerns our clients may have. Oftentimes, it's that time spent prior to doing the actual hoof work that is the most valuable to the horse owner. I also find that when it comes to a game plan to help the horse, any time spent listening to the horse owner and then discussing things, often leads the way to a discovery. Certain hoof problems, such as sole bruising, abscessing, or hoof wall cracking, may appear to have simple fixes, however even the simplest of conditions can be a hint of a deeper issue.

Recently, I was introduced to a 15 yr. old thoroughbred mare, retired from the race track and now being reconditioned for Eventing/Jumping. At first glance it seemed like a typical situation. The client had noticed some bruising on the soles of the front feet and could also feel the horse's discomfort when riding on harder surfaces. As I continued to visit with the horse and discuss more details with the owner, she casually mentioned that one foot seemed to show more signs of stress than the others. The foot that was more discolored from bruising happened to be white and was often labeled by others as " just a weakness that *all* white feet have". However, over the years, I've become more critical and feel that there is always an underlying reason for any asymmetrical hoof discoloration/ bruising, regardless of hoof pigmentation. Upon further examination of the horse, it became obvious that the situation was actually a result of an asymmetrical conformation in general.

When the owner began to realize the "bigger-picture", she seemed relieved and summarized it best—"It's amazing what I can learn about my horse when I begin to *look* at him, instead of just seeing him".

To me that just about says it all— as the best advice you could give to any farrier and/or horse owner, when they are attempting to solve many of those inconvenient hoof problems.

With this "Farrier-Friendly"™ guide my goal is to help you gain a better awareness of your horse and how his hooves are influenced. A basic understanding of a situation is always the best place to start when confronted with any sort of problem— especially when it pertains to your horse's hoof.

Thank you for your interest in "Farrier-Friendly"™ and good luck as you continue your journey of learning with your horse.

Your friend in horses,

Bryan Farcus MA,CJF-BWFA

A healthy hoof is one that includes hard, solid soles

and soft, flexible frog bands with a triangular center.

The outer hoof wall should be at least two times

greater than the width of the white line, and the white

line should bond with no deep cracks between the

connecting sole.

Common Problems:
●1. A "frog-eating" bacterium called *thrush* can
cause bleeding, soreness, or even death if not attended
to.
●2. Weak cracking of outside wall due to extremely
wet or dry conditions. Horses have a great capacity to
adapt to environmental changes. However, it must be
gradual. Sometimes horses need a little help.

●3. Sole bruising often results from constant, misuse
of horses on rocky uneven surfaces. If soles are
tender, find out whether the cause is heredity (flat-
soled) or environmental (ground being too wet, which
softens soles or too rough and rocky).

●4. Limb interference or hitting may result from
unbalanced riding, lack of shoeing and trimming,
and/or fatigue of horse.

Common Solutions:

●1. Thrush can be prevented or treated by practicing good "hoof hygiene". A pick a day will be a very small price to pay. Advanced cases of thrush are life threatening to your horse so time is of the essence. Some common solutions can range from natural to commercial. On the natural side, vinegars or borax powder may be helpful. Commercial options include copper sulfate based solutions, peroxides, or chlorine water.

●2. Weak, "brittle" foot cracking can be helped by adding an oil-based hoof dressing. Weak, "soft" feet can be improved by using hoof hardening conditioners (such as, home remedies like pine tar/ turpentine solutions or commercial products like *Keratex* or *Tuff Stuff*). Some cases may also benefit from an oil-based hoof dressing that acts as a repellent of water.

●3. Sole bruising is a remedy for "Father Time". Rest is best. Hoof padding under shoes is not a cure, but a prevention. Pads provide protection against potential bruising. Pads may have extreme negative effects if put on an existing bruised horse, as the concentrated pressure of a pad may be too much to bear.

●4. Interfering limbs can be helped with improved riding skill, conditioning of the horse, and routine farrier work. Protective boots are recommended during these times of need.

When to call a Farrier?
Generally, most horses, whether shod or not, should have the farrier call on them routinely. Most farriers recommend anywhere from 6-8 weeks varying among each horse and each season. Most healthy horses can be barefoot if they are in a controlled environment. Some may need shoes for any of these (3) reasons:
1) weak hooves (protection)
2) weak hoof/pastern angles (support)
3) the job of the horse (performance)

A good farrier should also consider this:
1) what science wants (for soundness)
2) what the rider/driver wants (for performance)
3) and what the horse wants (for a lifetime of humane horseshoeing and handling in general)

Finally, the farrier you choose should have a professional level of National Certification (i.e. AFA, BWFA, AAPF). This choice can be hard. I suggest you listen to your horse and not exclusively on comments from your "horse-friends".

It's also worth remembering this timeless creed…

"A consistently sound horse is a farrier's walking billboard."

Whether your horse lives mainly at pasture or in a stable, there's one concern that always creeps up. At some point, whether it is seasonal or randomly reoccurring, your horse may develop a foul odor emitting from his frogs. That stench is most assuredly a frog-eating, anaerobic bacterium called "thrush". Since this bacterial disease is anaerobic, it survives without the presence of oxygen. In fact, oxygen will actually kill it. In many minor cases, just a hoof picking a day will be enough to keep thrush away. As I often explain to my students, the conditions that accelerate thrush are conceptually relative to those that accelerate tooth decay within our teeth. When was the last time you heard of a person dying from a case of tooth decay? Sounds quite absurd doesn't it? Unfortunately, I have heard of horses being put down due to advanced cases of thrush. My point, here, is

simple. Thrush (frog decay) and cavities (tooth

decay) are both hygiene-related issues and they are

both very easily prevented.   The other good news, in

all of this, is that most studies suggest that minor

cases of thrush have approximately a three day

window to arrive and a three day window to

disappear, provided that appropriate measures are

taken.

What are the structures involved?—The *frog* and its

two distinct layers—The external skin is called *horn*

tissue and the corresponding vascular layer of tissue is

called the *sensitive corium*. Beneath the inner

sensitive layer lies a pad-like, shock absorber that

reduces concussion for the horse's hoof and his entire

limb called the *deep digital cushion*.

The initial signs will be rather obvious, starting at the

deep crevices of the frog (*sulci*), black puss-like discharge accompanied by a foul odor will be present.

Five Simple Steps can make a Big Difference...

When battling a minor case of thrush, remember to:

- ☑ Underline Debride. Pick and clean out hoof. Scoop out the easily removable "shedding" tissue. A hoof pick with a built-in brush is very handy. Any partially torn edges of frog tissue should be removed with a hoof knife. (if you're unsure, ask your farrier or vet for some assistance) .

- ☑ Disinfect. There are many disinfectants available on the market. Some common "wet" solutions are: Formula Solution™, Thrush Buster™, Kopertox™, Huuf Magic™, and Thrush Be Gone™ . Of course, for minor cases, I've found that a simple and cost effective solution is to mix[11] 50% Clorox bleach and 50% water into a twist top or sports top bottle, which can be used as a routine hoof wash. One word of caution, too much bleach could hurt the healthy tissue, so don't over-do your mix.

☑ <u>Make a Date</u>. Don't forget to have your farrier out to trim on a routine basis. One of the leading causes of thrush can be due to over growth of the frog tissue that may not shed as efficiently as it should; this can cause bacteria to be trapped in and around the frog.

☑ <u>Make Adjustments</u>. It may be necessary to change your horse's living conditions from time-to-time. Giving him a break from a stall or moving him from a mucky paddock

into a bigger area with fewer pools of
concentrated mud, can make all the
difference.

☑ <u>Be Diligent.</u> Re-assess the problem
regularly. Depending on the season, your
horse may be more prone to contract thrush.
In many cases, symptoms can appear within
three days, leading to a well established case
of thrush. The good news—it can disappear
just as quickly.

Is it more than minor?...

What about the major cases, you ask? They would be
cases where thrush bacteria invade the sensitive layers
of the frog. It is common in these cases to see
bleeding of the frog as well. Your farrier and/or vet
will most generally ask you to move your horse into a
clean, dry area and prescribe an antiseptic foot wash

with betadine solution or a foot soak with warm

Epsom salt water.   Afterwards, if bleeding still

persists, you will need to apply a temporary bandage.

One word of caution, in these cases, it's always a

good idea to confer with your vet. He or she will

most likely suggest that your horse be updated

on his tetanus shots. Once the healing of the frog

begins, it would be wise to maintain a "cleanliness-

first" policy for your horse's feet. Remember that

regardless of the type of thrush medication you

choose, it will be most effective when administered

directly after a thorough hoof cleaning.

- There are a variety of commercial grade thrush

  solutions on the market these days. They range

  from the more traditional "wet" solutions, which

  are liquid based, or as a "dry ", powder solution.

  The treatment approach you choose will depend

on the severity of your horse's thrush condition.
For the more stubborn thrush cases, the application of a dry formula can make all the difference.   For years, many horsemen would rely on home-remedy "dry" concoctions, such as lime dust, borax powder or copper sulfate. Today, with an increase in innovative horse care products, the use of dry formula treatments is, once again, becoming popular.   One product that I have experimented with and have had some success is a product labeled as *No Thrush (Four Oaks Products).* In any given situation, there seems to be a degree of experimentation, which I suspect, will never change and it will continue to be the job of the equine professional to keep informed and, when the opportunity arises, be willing to educate.

Becoming more 'Abscess Aware'...

Sometimes anticipation of a problem can be worse than the problem itself. When it comes to your horse and his potential for hoof injury this statement couldn't be more fitting, and for that reason I offer this advice.

Step #1- Understand Hoof Form and Function:
The horse's hoof is unique in many respects. When you do a little research, the first thing most equine anatomy books are quick to point-out is the continuous influence that the environment will have on your horse. Horses have been credited for being the most adaptable species known to man and, in actuality, the decisions we make are the essence of the horse's environment. Therefore, many of the hoof problems we encounter are, oftentimes, the net result of the husbandry (level of care) that has been given to the horse. And, it's been said that "good husbandry for a horse's hooves is like what good hygiene is for a person's teeth." Being observant and addressing minor problems will, in the vast majority of cases,

result in satisfactory solutions. Unfortunately, on some occasions a mystifying lameness will suddenly appear, as though it had happened overnight. A hoof abscess or *gravel,* as some call it, almost always greets us in this manner. To fully understand this process, let's review the form, as well as the function of your horse's foot.

Although most scientific matters seem complicated, they can be simplified if you realize that there are many related features between the horse's body and our own. In fact, we are so anatomically similar that most medical journals rely on the same numerical notations to describe the arrangement of bones for both the horse, as well as the human. Also, on somewhat of an interesting note, recent studies suggest that, even though the human newborn starts out with approximately 270 "soft" bones, both mature human and horse end-up with approximately 205 permanent bones. When it comes to the horse's hoof structure, we can relate certain similarities to our finger and toe nail structure. For instance, any nutritional disturbances in your system (or your horse's) will result in an altered form of the body's basic external properties (i.e. the skin, hair, hooves or nails). So perhaps, metaphorically speaking, we <u>are</u> what we <u>eat</u>.

Beginning to familiarize yourself with the connective tissue layers within your horse's hoof is the first step toward understanding its function and any possible malfunction.

In many instances, anecdotal explanations allow us to utilize our imagination, so that we can comprehend more complex concepts. Such is the case, here, when examining the mechanics of the hoof. Imagine the following five essential hoof functions as though they were interchangeable parts within a "well-tuned" machine:

- ♦ Function (#1) --To bear the weight of the horse.
- ♦ Function (#2) --To provide traction
- ♦ Function (#3) --To protect from any negative environmental elements
- ♦ Function (#4) --To absorb concussion
- ♦ Function (#5) --To facilitate circulation of blood throughout the lower extremities.

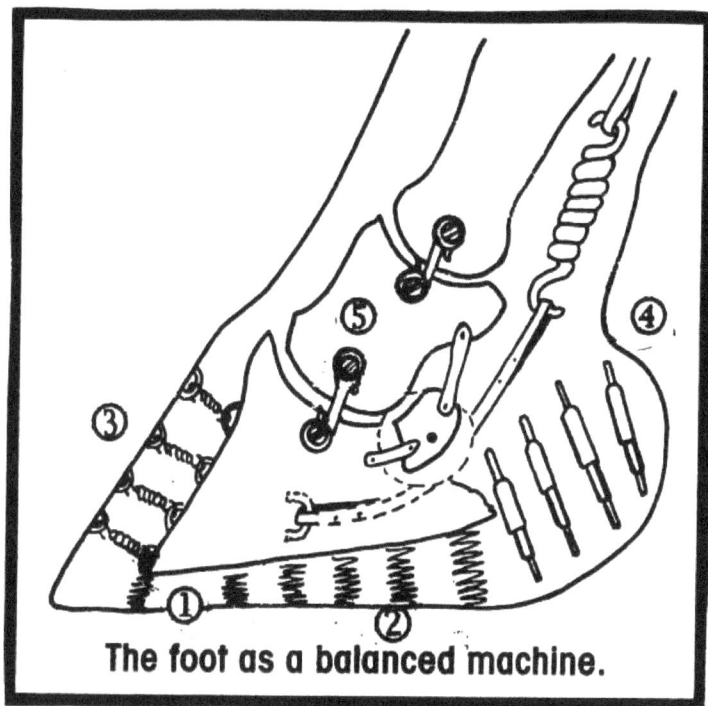

The foot as a balanced machine.

Illustration courtesy of Ric Redden, DVM

Step #2- Classify The Injury:

Now that you've established a familiarity with the hoof structures and function, let's discuss one of the most common hoof injuries. According to the seventh edition of the The Merck Veterinary Manual, a hoof abscess is the leading cause of lameness for most horses and it can result from any one of these three situations:

(1) A ***mild bruising*** of the sensitive tissue beneath the exposed layers of the hoof is usually identified by the presence of reddish discoloration. This commonly occurs in the sole region of the hoof and is evidence of a subcutaneous hemorrhage in that area. Since the bleeding of this tissue is minor and , oftentimes, well on its way to healing itself before it becomes noticeable, it is often referred to as a "<u>dry</u>" injury.

(2) A ***Moderate friction-related*** irritation to the horse's sole or frog can create a pool of serum beneath these areas, much like a blister on the base of your foot. Many veterinarians will label this a "<u>moist</u>" injury.

And(3) The ***most severe, a "suppurating"*** ***injury***. With this type of injury a necrosis (death) of the sensitive tissues within the sole and/or digital cushion will occur. In such instances, an obstruction or puncture wound is usually present, allowing infection to set-in and "puss-pockets" to develop. Pressure will build inside the infected hoof and the horse will be in great pain, leaving him "three-legged" lame, so to speak.

Nature of the Beast...

Being observant and addressing minor concerns will, in the vast majority of cases, prevent the occurrence of many hoof complications. However, despite all your efforts, one day you may enter your barn and be shocked to find your horse in a helpless posture, as he struggles to move and can not bear any weight on one of his hooves. You instantly entertain thoughts of a broken leg or a ruptured tendon. Fortunately, after some investigating, you breathe a sigh of relief, as you rule out these extreme possibilities. But, what now? What lameness could be so mystifying, as though it had happened overnight? The answer: Hoof abscess. An abscess or *gravel*, as some call it, almost always greets us in this manner. When a horse's hoof tissue is damaged to a degree that penetrates the deeper, sensitive tissue, foreign material (most likely gravel) can enter and cause sepsis (infection). The pain experienced by the horse will often leave him "three-legged" lame.

Earlier Detection...

According to most veterinary manuals, a hoof abscess is the leading cause of hoof related lameness. Generally speaking, abscesses will manifest in one of three situations:

❶ A bruising of the sole (*dry injury)* is usually visible as a reddish discoloration which occurs due to a minor subcutaneous bleed. Often, when we see the discoloration the healing process has already begun and most likely the horse is showing no sign of lameness.

❷ Weakening of tissue due to over-exposure to

moisture (*moist injury*), causing fissures (cracks) on [22] the surface of sole, which provides the opportunity for a friction-related irritation and/or hoof wall separation.

❸ An obstruction/ puncture of the sole or frog which generates necrosis (death) of the infected sensitive tissue (*suppurating injury*); often this injury is unable to be treated without veterinary assistance, since the puncture can be deep within the coria (sensitive structures). Also, if the object of puncture (nail, wire, long wood splinter) is still lodged within the hoof, you should resist temptation and DO NOT remove until your veterinarian is consulted.

Prevention...

And finally, keep in mind that prevention of an abscess is primarily centered on eliminating any possible source, such as:

- ° dropped nails along fence line or barn area after repairs/ an attractor magnet is very helpful.
- ° roadside, tossed glass bottles or aluminum cans.
- ° buried barbed wire from older fence lines.

Also, equally important is to commit to a regular farrier schedule. An experienced farrier will be able to spot the early symptoms that may predispose your horse to an abscess. Quite often, in this situation, many people tend to overlook the benefits of a well-balanced hoof. In my practice, I've noticed that there tends to be a strong correlation between neglected, unbalanced hooves and the reoccurrence of abscesses.

You can understand certain Hoof Problems by noticing Limb Length Disparity (*LLD*)...

BELOW: a view of a balanced and symmetrical top-line.

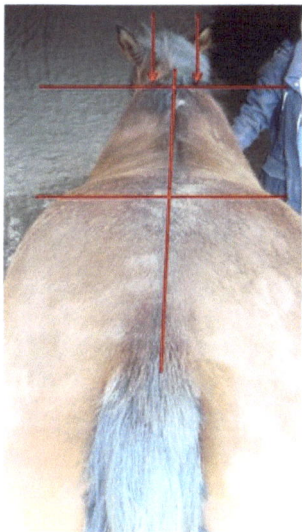

Photo by: Bryan S. Farcus   Learning to view your horse's top-line can offer you a better understanding of why the feet are as they are. Using a top-down approach to assess hoof balance can help a farrier make better trimming and shoeing decisions.

NEXT PAGE (below): a view of a typical dropped shoulder/ but this horse is functionally sound ,as long as he is trimmed and shod to support and promote a more balanced top-line, as opposed to corrective shoeing for the hooves only.

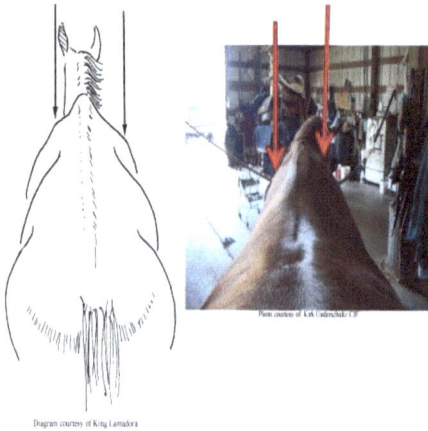

Diagram courtesy of Kirig Llamadora

[Above-]: Before

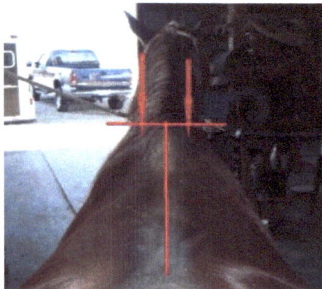

[Above-]: same horse: After

Top-line imbalances can result due to a variety of conformational issues.   Of the most common are: *Club footedness, Low-underrun heels, Curvature of the spine, Dropped shoulder/or hip, Congenital bone length differences within limbs.* Some are functional deviations while others are not.

Glossary of Terms:

Axis BB (Broken-Back): hoof to pastern digit axis line that is visualized to represent a long toe/low heel hoof conformation.

Axis BF (Broken-Forward): hoof to pastern digit axis line that is visualized to represent a short toe/high heel hoof conformation.

Bars: viewed from the bottom of the hoof, minor protrusions present on both sides of the frog, a connective tissue that ties the buttress of the heel to the sole, acts to reinforce the heels.

Bar shoe: general term used to indicate any shoe that is closed or connected at the ends to maximize weight bearing surface, often used to stabilize a weak hoof or support a weakness in a limb.

BBLS: (Basic Body Language System) a term used to identify any system of communicating with the horse through herd instincts, based on predetermined gestures, signals, or cues that are horse logical.

Bulb: located at the back of a hoof connecting the frog and the coronary band, often referred to as the frog band.

Buttress of Heel: the part of the hoof wall that runs to the open end of the foot, often referred to as the point or butt of the heel.

Conformation: an overall view of the horse's entire body, comparing the horse's body structure for symmetry and/or functional alignment.

Commissures: the grooves that are present on either side of the frog, sometimes referenced as the paracuneal sulci.

Corrective shoeing: an approach to shoeing with a major emphasis on changing the horse's stance and/or way of going.

Coronary Band: a band of soft tissue that surrounds the top of each hoof nearest the hairline.

Club footed: a hoof that grows excessively high in the heel as compared to the toe length, there are various degrees of severity, generally considered "clubby" if the horse's hoof-to-pastern is broken-forward, due to a flexor tendon contracture that is extreme enough to distend the coffin joint. This condition may be due to an injury, but most commonly inherited.

Deep Digital Cushion: also know as the plantar cushion, a fibro-fatty tissue underlying the frog that functions as a shock absorber.

Degree Pad: wedged shaped pads that are placed between the hoof and the shoe that will raise the hoof and lift the rear surface of a limb.

Deviation: a departure from a predetermined ideal, a term often used in horse conformation analysis to describe crookedness in a limb.

Dynamic Hoof Balance: evaluation of hoof balance as it pertains to the horse in motion, considering how the hoof will land and load.

Frog: a triangular shaped, elastic pad-like tissue that is located at the bottom of the foot that acts to absorb concussion and aid in traction

Gait: a pattern of movement or the way in which the horse travels, certain gaits are natural to all horses but some can be artificial.

Hoof Anatomy: the study of the structure/parts of a hoof.

Hoof Physiology: the study of the function of a hoof.

Interfering: a term used to describe the hitting together of a horse's foot to an opposing limb in a manner that restricts the horse's ability to move forward in a comfortable manner.

Keratination: a process whereby the division of horn producing cells accumulate to produce outer layers of hoof wall to protect sensitive tissue, similar to our own nail growth.

LLD (Limb Length Disparity): a condition where the horse suffers from a structural difference of his limbs as a working pair, often a curvature of the spine and/or a clubbed footed conformation is present.

Low-Underrun Heels: When viewed from the side, the heels of the horse are collapsed and low to the ground, the slope or angle of the heel is much lower than that of the toe.

Phalanx -1st : the first bone in the lower limb directly below the fetlock, also known as the long pastern.

Phalanx -2nd: the second bone in the lower limb directly below the fetlock, also known as the short pastern.

Phalanx -3rd: the third and last bone in the lower limb directly below the fetlock, also known as the coffin bone.

Quarter: when viewed from the bottom of the hoof, the region of hoof wall that is between the toe and heel.

Sensitive Laminae: an interlocking, velcro-like tissue within a hoof that is responsible for connecting the hoof wall to the coffin bone.

Seat of corn: viewed from the bottom of the hoof, a junction where the edge of the bar, sole and white-line come together, an area susceptible to attracting debris that can result in a sore spot (corn).

Sole: the flat, ground surface portion of the hoof, responsible for creating a natural pad that is designed to protect the coffin bone.

Static Hoof Balance: a view of hoof balance when the horse is at a stand still, using a geometric reference (X,Y,Z planes) for a three dimensional perspective.

Supportive Shoeing: fitting a shoe with enough length and width to protect and support the entire limb.

Therapeutic Shoeing: an approach to shoeing that provides a level of comfort and also attempts to remedy a hoof disease.

Vertical Depth Tolerance: a general reference to the amount of exfoliated sole that is able to be safely trimmed without causing the horse to be tender.

White line: usually yellowish or brown, it is the connective tissue (terminal ends of the sensitive laminea) that bonds the hoof wall to the sole, aids in nail placement.

Helpful Tables & Graphics:

This page is reprinted with permission from the
Author of

HORSE FOOT CARE
By Dr. Doug Butler

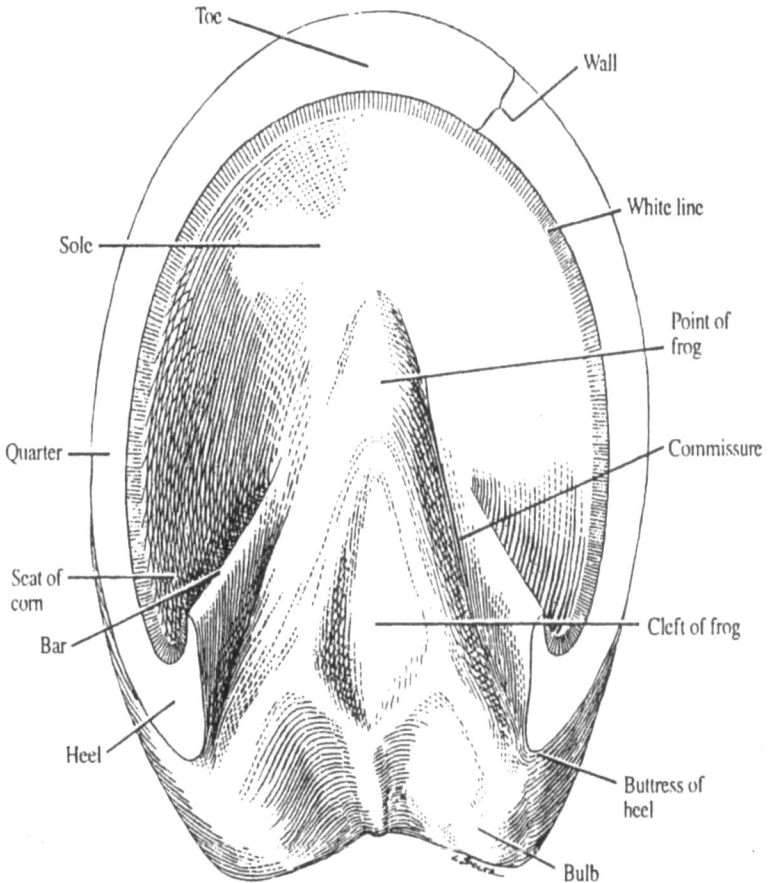

The parts of the hoof

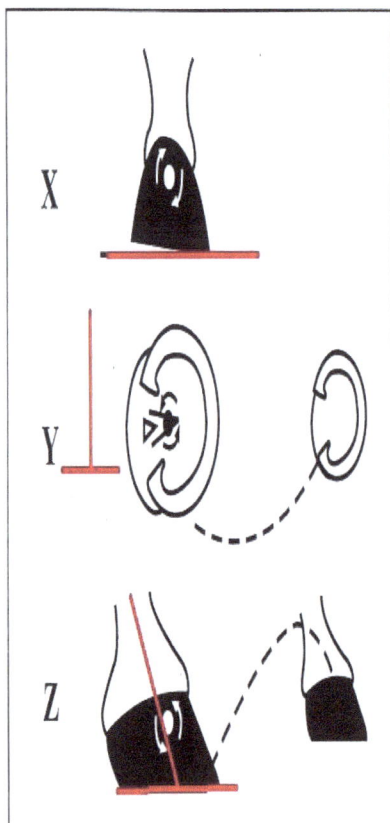

Visualing the 3 dimensions of balance as applied to Dynamic or Functional balance.

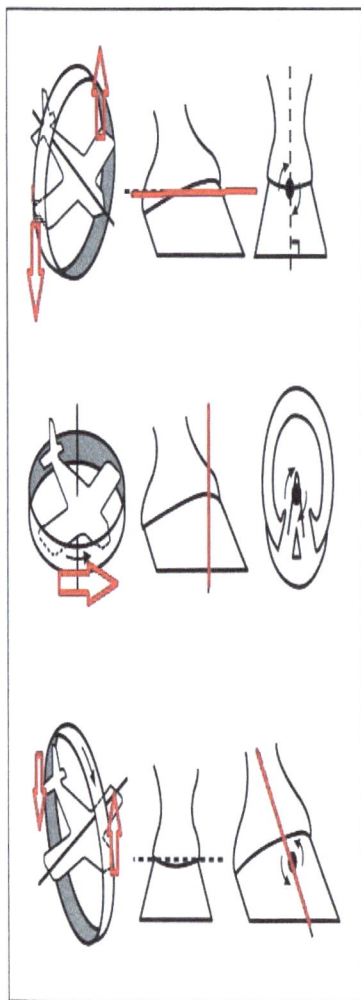

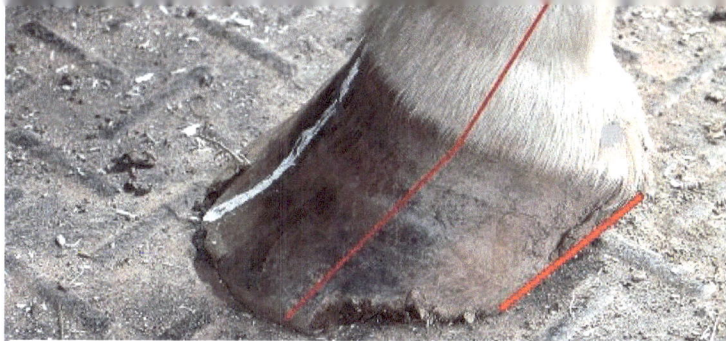

Broken-Back Axis

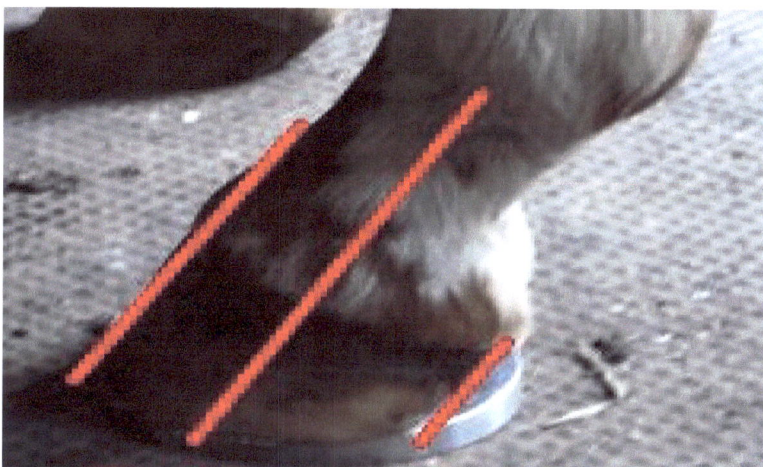

Balanced

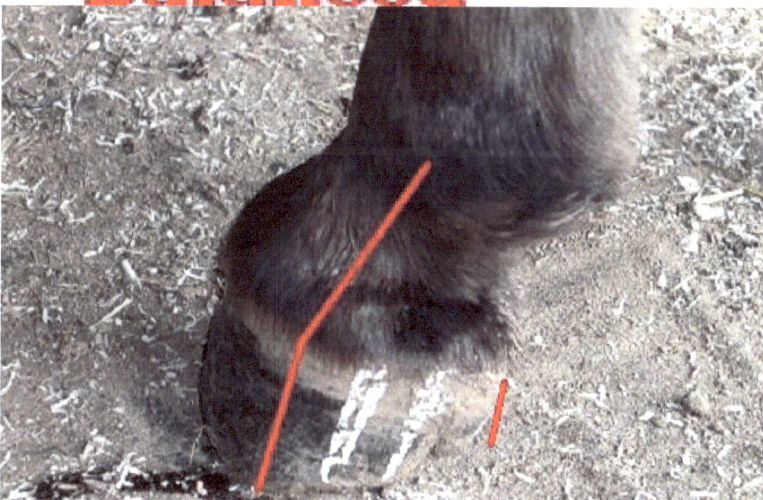

Broken-Forward Axis

Photos by: Bryan Farcus CJF

A POSITIVE *"A Healthy Hoof"*	ITS OPPOSITE *"An Unhealthy Hoof"*
Hard/shiny exterior hoof wall.	Soft/cracked, dull exterior wall.
Symmetrically shaped hoof wall.	Asymmetrically shaped hoof wall.
Soft/flexible hair line tissues.	Hard/"crusty" hair line tissues.
Soft/flexible frog tissues.	Hard or diseased frog tissues.
Parallel growth pattern of toe and heel lengths.	Reversed growth pattern of toe and heel lengths.
Normal cupping of the sole. (bottom surface of hoof is arched allowing for edge of hoof wall to contact ground first)	Extremely flat or "dropped" sole. (bottom surface of hoof is contacting the ground before edge of hoof wall)
Hoof wall thickness approx. 2 x greater than "white line" thickness.	Hoof wall thickness less than the "white line" thickness (white line distortion)
"White line" region and sole surface adjoin without deep cracks present.	Deep cracks existing between the "white line" region and the sole surface.

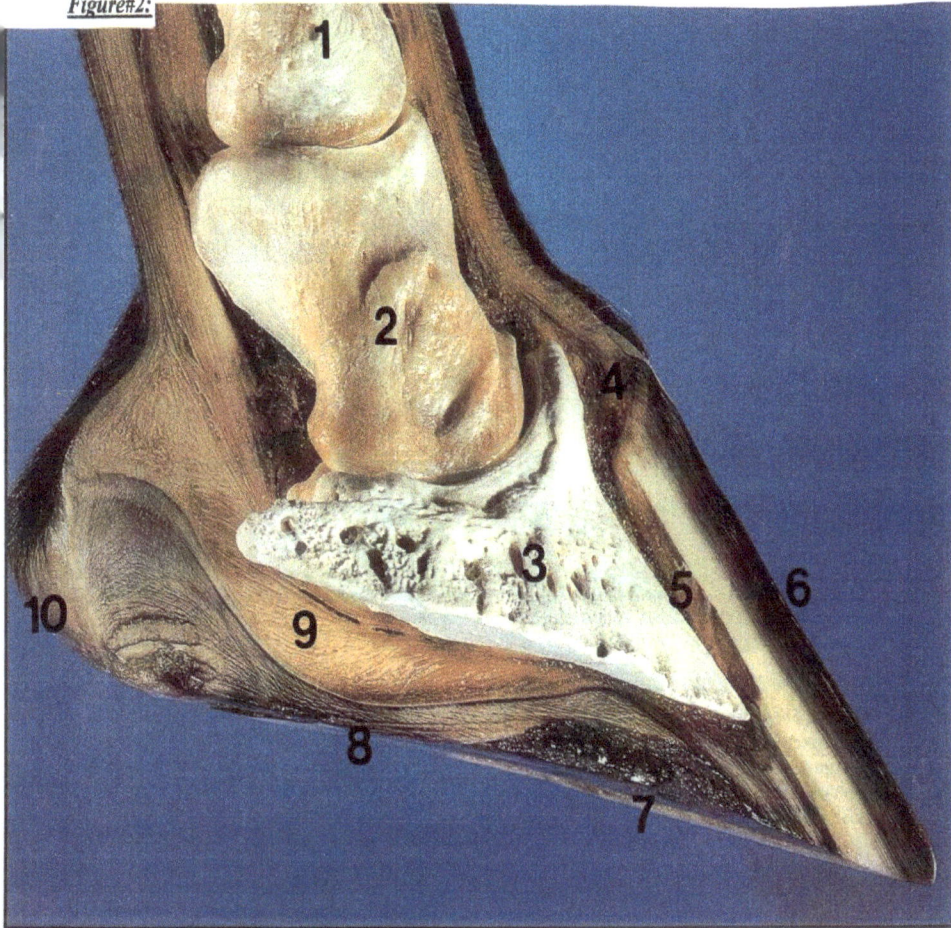

LATERAL OBLIQUE VIEW OF EQUINE DIGIT. Soft tissue is removed from one side of the phalanges.

Used by permission, courtesy of : The American Farriers Journal, ©1999 Lessiter Publications, Inc.

1. First Phalanx (long pastern).
2. Second Phalanx (short pastern).
3. Third Phalanx (coffin bone).
4. Coronary Band.
5. Sensitive Laminae.
6. Hoof wall (toe region).
7. Sole.
8. Frog.
9. Deep Digital Cushion.
10. Bulb of foot.

RESOURCES...

American Farrier's Journal, Lessiter Publications

PBM : A Diary of Lameness, Anthony Gonzales

Shoeing In Your Right Mind , Dr. Doug Butler

Horseowner's Guide to Lameness, Dr. Ted Stashsak

The Principles of Horseshoeing (P3),Doug &Jacob Butler

The Lame Horse , James R. Rooney DVM

WEBSITES...

www.nanric.com
www.reddendvm.com

ASSOCATIONS...

AAPF, American Association of Professional Farriers,
www.professionalfarriers.com

AFA, American Farrier's Association,
www.americanfarriers.org

BWFA, Brotherhood of Working Farriers,
www.bwfa.net

About The Author :

Bryan S. Farcus MA, CJF-BWFA ~

For the past 25 years, Bryan has been combining the skills of horseshoeing, teaching, and riding. He is a Certified Journeyman Farrier through the Brotherhood of Working Farriers Association (BWFA) and also holds a certification in Equine Massage Therapy. Bryan's other accomplishments include both a Master of Arts degree with a specialization in equine education and a Bachelor of Science degree in the area of business.

For more than ten years, Bryan was the director/ instructor of a Farrier Studies program at an international equestrian college and a guest instructor for others, as well.

These days, he continues his teaching by offering various "horsemanship for horseshoeing" programs. Upon invitation, Bryan presents demonstrations and group discussions on basic hoof care and horsemanship, in order to promote the advancement of equine education. Bryan is also the creator of a select line of "*Farrier-Friendly*™" products and currently authors a series of "*Farrier-Friendly*™" articles that appear in horse magazines throughout the US. Bryan currently works with horses and their owners in Ohio and West Virginia. You can visit him at:

www.farrierfriendly.com or e-mail: farrierfriendly@hotmail.com